Contents

Some words are printed in bold, **like this**. You can find out what they mean by looking in the glossary.

Meet the family!

Welcome to my family album! Let me introduce you to some of my relatives. Maybe you've met some of us before?

Cats can sleep for 12 to 18 hours a day! But they're often awake during the night.

You'll find cats all over the world. Some live in homes with humans, while others are wild. Cats first started living with people around 5,000 years ago. They helped keep rats and mice away from grain stores. The ancient Egyptians even worshipped cats as gods!

One big family

There are so many different types of cat, but they're all part of the same family. Some are big, some are small, some are fluffy, and some are deadly, but they all have certain things in common. If you have a pet cat you'll already know how much they love to play and sleep. But what else do cats get up to?

Cats in the wild sleep a lot, too. They need to save their energy for hunting.

A day in our life

It's natural for all cats to want to hunt for food. In the wild, cats can spend up to eight hours every day hunting. Pet cats get food from their owners, but they still have the **instinct** to hunt. You can see this when kittens learn to chase and pounce on toys.

All cats need to eat meat to stay healthy. They also need to drink plenty of water.

Cats like to stay clean. We wash ourselves with our tongues several times a day, especially after we eat.

FAMILY SECRET

Whiskers don't just look good, they help cats to hunt. Whiskers feel **vibrations** when **prey** is moving near by. They also help cats to find their way around and judge if a space is big enough for them to fit through.

Keep out!

All cats like to have their own space or **territory**. They like to keep other cats out! Some cats mark their territory by scratching, so it's a good idea to get a pet cat a scratching post. In the wild, cats scratch or mark trees to leave a smell that warns other cats to stay away.

Lots of pet cats have short hair. Let's leap into the album and find out about some of these **breeds**.

The American Shorthair is the most popular pet cat in the United States.

American Shorthair cats

The first American Shorthair cats are supposed to have travelled to North America with European settlers. This strong, slim cat has thick, short hair and is friendly and active. They make great pets and are known for catching mice! American Shorthair cats can have coats with different colours and patterns, such as tabby, tortoiseshell, and ginger. Tabby patterns can be striped or spotted. Most tortoiseshell cats are female, with different coloured patches on their fur.

Abyssinian cats

Abyssinian cats are slender and **agile**. They have beautiful almond-shaped eyes, large ears, and soft, glossy coats. Abyssinian cats are active and curious, and love to explore. They make great pets because they are clever and have a sweet nature. They are usually happy to play with their owners.

FAMILY SECRET

A breed is a group of cats with distinctive characteristics. These characteristics can include the way a cat behaves and the way it looks.

Abyssinian cats can look like they're walking on tiptoes because of their long, slim legs.

Soft and sleek

These shorthaired cats from different parts of the world are both famous for their beautiful fur and unusual eyes.

Those beautiful blue eyes don't see as well in the dark as other cats' eyes, so Siamese cats can be less active at night.

Siamese cats

Siamese cats come from Southeast Asia. They have long, sleek bodies and slim legs. Their fur is usually a pale colour, with a darker head, feet, and tail. Their blue eyes and very pointed ears make them stand out from the crowd! Siamese cats are clever and love lots of attention. They can get very noisy if you don't play with them!

Russian Blue cats

Russian Blue cats' silvery-blue fur is soft and shimmery and their green eyes are stunning. Russian Blue cats are elegant and slim, with a long tail and delicate legs. Unlike Siamese cats, Russian Blues can be quiet and shy with people until they get used to them.

FAMILY SECRET

Siamese and Russian Blue cats both have links with royalty! The royal family in Thailand kept Siamese cats for centuries, while a Russian **Tsar** had a favourite Russian Blue called Vashka!

Russian Blue cats are from Russia, where they are considered to be good luck.

What's missing?

Both these **breeds** are missing things that most cats have. Can you spot what they haven't got?

Manx cats make a sweet trilling noise when they communicate with their kittens.

Manx cats

Manx cats come from a small island off the northwest coast of England, called the Isle of Man. Many Manx kittens are born with no tail, or a very short, stumpy tail. These cats are strong and sturdy with rounded bodies. Their back legs are longer and more powerful than the front legs, making them good at jumping! Manx cats make gentle and friendly pets.

Like humans, Sphynx cats have to be careful in the sun in case they get sunburn.

FAMILY SECRET

Sphynx cats get their name from a **mythical** creature called a sphinx. It had a lion's body, a bird's wings, and a woman's face.

Sphynx cats

Sphynx cats look like they've got no hair but in fact they've just got incredibly short hair! This breed started in Canada. Their coats can be different colours and patterns and look quite wrinkled. Sphynx cats also have very large ears and big eyes. They like to be cuddled, especially as this helps them to keep warm.

Big softies

Some members of my family have longer hair. Here are some of my cousins who need your help brushing their coats!

The cuddly-looking Persian enjoys being held and stroked by people.

Persian cats

Persian cats have the longest hair of all cats. This hair can be many different colours and is very thick. Persian cats have short legs and stocky bodies. Their round faces have snubbed noses between their eyes, giving them a "squashed" look! They are gentle and calm cats, so make good pets. But their owners need to be ready to comb that long hair every day!

Birman cats

People started keeping Birman cats in France in the 1920s. Birman cats are semi-longhaired and their coat is very soft and silky. They have striking blue eyes and bushy tails. Birman cats are known for their gentle, easygoing nature. Their fur needs to be brushed and combed a couple of times a week.

FAMILY SECRET

All Birman kittens are born with white fur. As they grow older, the fur on their legs, tail, face, and ears becomes darker, but their toes stay white.

Birman cats have long, stocky bodies and large paws.

Turkish Van cats

Turkish Van cats are a very old **breed** from southeastern Turkey. They are quite happy swimming in water and have a waterproof coating on their thick fur. Their coat is white, with markings on the head and fluffy tail. This active cat likes to run and play games. Turkish Van cats are happy around other pets but they don't like to be handled too much.

My relatives come from many countries. Here are two of my longhaired cousins who like water.

Turkish Van cats have thick fur for the cold weather. They can shed a lot of hair when it gets warm.

Norwegian Forest cats climb down trees in a spiral, head first!

FAMILY SECRET

Norwegian forest cats are thought to have been the Vikings' pets. In Viking legends, they are called *Skogkatt*, or fairy cats.

Norwegian Forest cats

Norwegian Forest cats come from the cold woodlands of Norway. Their fur is thick to cope with tough winters and is **water-resistant**. This sturdy, independent cat loves the outdoors and water – it might try to catch fish in streams and ponds! Norwegian Forest cats make clever, playful pets for people who live in the countryside.

These American cousins of mine are both big and fluffy and make very friendly pets!

Maine Coon cats may have got their name because their bushy tails and colouring reminded people of racoons.

Maine Coon cats

Maine Coon cats developed to survive cold winters, so they have heavy, thick coats and long, bushy tails. Maine Coon cats love the outdoors and sleep almost anywhere! They don't demand attention from their owners and like to have plenty of space. This easygoing cat doesn't need to be groomed more than once a week.

Maine Coon cats are the oldest **breed** of cat in North America. One story tells that cats belonging to an English sailor called Captain Charles Coon had kittens in the United States. These longhaired kittens became known as "Coon's cats".

Ragdoll cats

Ragdoll cats come from California. They got their name because they often become relaxed and floppy when you pick them up. They love to be held, and their fawn-coloured fur is soft and silky to stroke. Despite their floppiness, Ragdoll cats have powerful, muscular bodies and strong legs.

Ragdoll cats are sweet and cuddly and will usually let children play with them.

Lions in the family

> ROAR!
> That's one thing many big cats can do that your pet cat can't! Let's find out more about these wild hunters...

Just like pet cats, male lions like to mark their **territory**.

African lions

Many big cats like to live alone but African lions stick together in groups called **prides**. The females do most of the work. As well as looking after the cubs, they do the hunting. Working together as a team, they can hunt and kill big **prey** such as buffalo and wildebeest. Male lions are the only cats to have a mane. It takes about five years for the mane to grow.

Cougars can live in many different **habitats**, including mountains, deserts, and forests.

Cougars

Cougars live in North and South America and are also known as mountain lions or pumas. Unlike African lions, cougars like to live and hunt alone. Cougars have very strong back legs that help them to jump. They are good at **stalking** and **ambushing** their prey. They can hunt animals as big as elk and moose.

FAMILY SECRET

The term "big cats" can include lions, tigers, jaguars, leopards, cheetahs, and cougars. All big cats lie down to eat, while pet cats tend to crouch.

Spots and stripes

Leopards

Leopards are very good hunters, lying in wait for unsuspecting **prey**. Their spotted fur makes a very good **camouflage**. Leopards are excellent at climbing trees. They are strong enough to drag large prey up into a tree to hide it from other animals. They mainly live in Africa, but can still be found in parts of Asia.

The markings on a leopard's fur make it very hard to spot when it rests in a tree.

A tiger's stripes help to hide it as it **stalks** prey in the long grass.

FAMILY SECRET

You might not have heard of some of my spotted relatives. The clouded leopard is found in the forests of Southeast Asia, and the rare snow leopard lives in the mountains of Asia.

Tigers

The tiger is the largest of the big cats and also one of the most **endangered**. It mainly lives in Siberia and south Asia. Tigers need to eat a huge amount of food and have big, sharp teeth to help them do this. They're good swimmers, and when it's hot they like to cool off in rivers.

Our growing family

So you've met just a few of my many relatives. Now let me tell you about some of the youngsters in my family.

Young big cats, such as lions and tigers, are called cubs. Smaller cats have kittens. A pet cat will be pregnant for nine weeks before having kittens. Most cats have a **litter** of between two and seven kittens. Kittens' eyes and ears are closed for as long as two weeks after they are born.

Kittens and cubs survive on their mother's milk until they are old enough to eat meat.

Caring for cubs and kittens

Pet kittens need to stay with their mother for up to 12 weeks before they are ready to leave her. In a **pride** of lions, all the females have cubs at the same time and share the job of looking after them. Female big cats can carry their cubs around in their mouths! The cubs go limp so their mother's jaws can grip without hurting them.

Playing is a great way for a kitten to get to know its owner.

Help the family

Most cats don't belong to any particular **breed**. Most pet cats aren't **pedigrees**, but are a lovely mix of different cat types! Pedigree cats are expensive, can need a lot of attention, and may have health problems. Your average moggy can come in all colours, shapes, and sizes!

Every pet cat is different and has its own personality, but all cats need somewhere to scratch!

Rescue cats

Sadly, some pet cats are not looked after by their owners. Other cats have kittens that are not wanted. Luckily, there are rescue centres that take in and care for these cats. If you're thinking about getting a pet cat, a rescue centre could be a great place to start. Rescue centres make sure all the cats are healthy and check that any new owners can care for them properly.

Humans can help rescue cats by giving or raising money for rescue centres or **volunteering** to work there.

Rescue centres help new owners to adopt a cat who will suit their home and daily life.

27

What type of cat are you?

If you were a cat, what type would you be? Have a go at this quiz and find out!

1. What is your hair like?
a) Very short
b) Quite long and thick
c) Very long and needs lots of brushing!

2. How do you like to spend your free time?
a) Snuggled up under a blanket somewhere warm
b) Running around and playing
c) Lying around, relaxing

3. Do you like being the centre of attention?
a) You're happy when you're being cuddled
b) Yes, if you're playing games but you're not bothered about having attention all the time
c) Of course! You're beautiful and make sure everyone notices!

4. What do you do when you're near a pool?

a) Back away from all that cold water

b) Jump in and have a good swim!

c) Admire your reflection in the water

5. Do you like exploring the great outdoors?

a) No, it's either too cold or you could get sunburnt

b) Yes, it's great to run around in the space outside

c) You're happy staying in luxury indoors

Answers

Mostly a: you are a Sphynx cat! You are affectionate and clever and like cuddling up with your family in the warmth of your home.

Mostly b: you are a Turkish Van cat! You are very active and love to swim. You're friendly and clever, but you like to do your own thing when you feel like it.

Mostly c: you are a Persian cat! You have amazing hair but it takes a lot of work to keep it tangle-free! You're gentle and calm and like to hang out with the people you love.

Glossary

adopt take over the care of something or someone

agile able to move about quickly and easily

ambush lie in wait to attack

breed particular type of one kind of animal. For example, a Sphynx is a particular breed of cat. All the members of a breed are a similar size and shape, and they look alike.

camouflage colour, pattern, or texture of an animal's fur or skin that helps it to hide

communicate share information, ideas, or feelings with others

endangered in danger of dying out

habitat particular environment where a plant or animal lives

instinct natural need or behaviour that has not been learned

litter number of babies born at one time

mythical imaginary

pedigree from a family of purebred animals, with no mixing of different breeds

prey animal that is hunted and eaten by another animal

pride group of lions

reflex reaction or movement that happens without thinking

stalk creep after prey

territory area of land that an animal sees as its own space

Tsar title of the royal ruler in Russia up to 1917

unique one of a kind

vibration shaking movement

volunteer offering to give time and help for no pay

water-resistant able to keep away water

Find out more

Books

Battersea Dogs and Cats Home: Oscar's Story,
  (Red Fox, 2012)

Big Cats, Annabelle Lynch (Franklin Watts, 2012)

Cats (A Pet's Life), Anita Ganeri (Heinemann Library, 2009)

Mini Encyclopedia: Cats, Sarah Creese (Make Believe
  Ideas, 2011)

Websites

www.battersea.org.uk/cats/breeds
The Battersea Dogs and Cats Home website has lots of
information about different breeds of cat. You can also
find out more about caring for your cat.

www.bbc.co.uk/nature/life/Felidae
You can search on the BBC Nature website to find out
about different big cats.

www.rspca.org.uk/allaboutanimals/pets/cats
The RSPCA website is full of interesting facts about cats
and how to care for them.

www.wwf.org.uk
You can learn about endangered cats in the wild, such as
the tiger and snow leopard, on the WWF website.

Index